The Girls of the Good Day Orphanage

The Christmas
Dolls

by CAROL BEACH YORK

illustrated by Victoria de Larrea
cover illustration by John Speirs

A
LITTLE APPLE
PAPERBACK

SCHOLASTIC INC.

New York   Toronto   London   Auckland   Sydney

For my husband Dick,
with love

No part of this publication may be reproduced in whole or in
part, or stored in a retrieval system, or transmitted in any
form, or by any means, electronic, mechanical, photocopying,
recording, or otherwise, without written permission of the
publisher. For information regarding permission, write to
Scholastic Inc., 730 Broadway, New York, NY 10003.

ISBN 0-590-42435-1

12 11 10 9 8 7 6 5 4 3 2 1   3 4 5 6 7 8/9

Contents

The Christmas Dolls

It was two days before Christmas. A chilly December wind swept along the pavement and around the corners of Butterfield Square. The wind blew through the black iron fences. It blew hard against the doors of the old brick houses with their shiny brass doorknobs and against the windows with their little square panes.

Above the gate at Number 18, the sign that read THE GOOD DAY ORPHANAGE FOR GIRLS creaked in the wind. Inside, in the parlor, a fire burned in the fireplace.

Miss Lavender and Miss Plum were unpacking Christmas toys that had been sent from the clock factory across town. Every year at Christmastime the people who worked at the clock factory collected used toys, fixed them up as good as new, and sent them to places where Christmas presents were needed. Every year they sent a big box to Number 18 Butterfield Square.

Miss Lavender and Miss Plum had decided to light a fire in the fireplace because it was so close to Christmas. They had a good furnace in the basement to heat the house, but the fire would make the room cheerful and cozy. It was not a big roaring fire, for Miss Lavender and Miss Plum were careful not to use too much wood, but it gave a bright glow to the parlor.

This year, the Christmas toys sent to The Good Day were all dolls, one for every girl. When a rag doll named Florabelle was taken out of the big brown cardboard box, the first thing she saw was the fire sparkling behind the screen. Florabelle's eyes were clear green glass, and the fire made them shine.

"Oh, this one's only a rag doll," Miss Plum said.

"Oh, dear, so it is." Miss Lavender looked up over the top of her gold-rimmed glasses. Her face was flushed, warm and pink from bending over to take the dolls out of the big cardboard box. She was much shorter than Miss Plum and was round and plump, with a head full of soft, white curls. Miss Plum was thin and stood very straight, as though she had a ruler against her back. Her gray hair was tied up tight in a bun; no one had ever seen it any other way.

Miss Lavender and Miss Plum looked at Florabelle uncertainly. All the other dolls had smooth, hard pink heads and arms and legs. Some had eyes that opened and closed, and had hair that could be combed. But Florabelle was flat and limp, with yellow yarn braids, sewed-on glass eyes, and a mouth made of red darning thread.

"Well, anyway," Miss Plum said at last, "her dress is pretty."

"But she has no shoes," Miss Lavender said.

Miss Plum's attention was caught by the next doll she saw lying in the cardboard box, and she put Florabelle down.

"Look at this, Miss Lavender," she exclaimed as she took a small doll in a blue dress out of the box.

Poor Florabelle, who had felt very embarrassed to be stared at and talked about, forgot herself completely when she saw the doll that Miss Plum was now holding. The doll's face was very pretty, with eyes that opened and closed and a smiling mouth with tiny white teeth showing—but her head had been put on backward! And even worse—she had lost her hair! Her bald head gleamed as smooth as a pink Easter egg.

"Oh, *dear*!" said Miss Lavender.

"This doll was put in the box by mistake, it's plain to see," Miss Plum decided.

"I guess *so*," Miss Lavender agreed.

"Just look," Miss Plum said. "Head on backward. Wig gone."

"And *she* has no shoes, either," Miss Lavender murmured.

Florabelle looked at the other dolls lying along the window seat. They all had shoes, and some of them had stockings, too.

"Well, let's just set her aside for now," Miss Plum said. "Maybe we can fix her ourselves."

"Yes," said Miss Lavender, who always agreed with what Miss Plum said, "maybe we can."

Florabelle watched as Miss Plum set the bald-headed doll on top of a bookcase nearby. Miss Plum put the doll down so that her face was toward the wall, with the smooth, pink back of her head turned out to the room.

Oh, she can't see a thing, poor dear, Florabelle thought to herself, but there was nothing she could do to help.

One by one all the dolls were taken out of the box. And still Florabelle was the only rag doll with glass-button eyes and a thread mouth; the only doll (except the poor doll on the bookcase) without shoes.

In a corner of the room, a Christmas tree stood ready to be trimmed, and on the floor beside the tree a box of ornaments was open. Long strands of silver tinsel spilled out over the carpet. The sofa by the fireplace was piled high with angel costumes, their thin white material covering the cushions. As the clock on the mantel ticked along toward three o'clock, Miss Plum looked up several times.

"We must have the dolls wrapped by three-fifteen," she reminded Miss Lavender, "because the girls are coming then to try on the costumes."

Yes," said Miss Lavender, "we must hurry."

One by one they put each Christmas doll in a layer of white tissue paper and then a layer of pretty red- and green-Christmas paper. They tied up each package with red ribbon pulled from a large spool on the table by the window seat. The dolls talked among themselves as they waited to be wrapped, which was all right, of course—Miss Plum and Miss Lavender could not hear dolls talk.

The dolls were all so happy to be fixed up as good as new again and to be going to little girls who would play with them and love them.

"I've been up in an attic for three years," one doll said, sighing with delight. "It's wonderful to see something besides storage boxes and cobwebs again. Look at the Christmas tree! Look at the snow!"

"Yes, yes, see the snow!" all the other dolls called out happily. And indeed, a light snow had just begun to fall. It whirled across Butterfield Square in the wind. "Look, Miss Plum. We will have snow for Christmas after all," said Miss Lavender.

Miss Plum looked out at the snow. "I think that calls for another log, don't you, Miss Lavender?"

"Oh, yes, indeed I do." Miss Lavender got up and put another piece of wood into the fire. The fire flared up, crackling and dancing. "Isn't it lovely?"

Miss Plum watched the fire a moment, nodding with satisfaction. Then she said, "But just look at the clock, Miss Lavender! We must be done by three-fifteen."

So on they went, wrapping the dolls in a layer of tissue paper and then a layer of Christmas paper, tying them up tightly with the red ribbon.

"I've got a new dress and bonnet," one of the dolls said.

"They gave me new hair," said another.

The dolls were nearly all wrapped, when suddenly Miss Plum dropped the tissue paper she was holding and said, "Wait a minute, Miss Lavender — they've sent too many."

"Oh?" Miss Lavender said. She looked up, holding her finger on the bow she was tying.

Miss Plum counted the dolls out loud. "...twenty-five, twenty-six, twenty-seven, twenty-eight, twenty-*nine*! Just as I thought. There's one extra."

"Twenty-*nine*?" Miss Lavender said. "You're right, Miss Plum. One extra. In fact," she added with dismay, "two extra." She nodded over to the bookcase where the bald doll sat staring at the wall.

Miss Plum looked at the dolls and tried to

decide what to do. At last she picked up Florabelle and said, "Let's just set this one aside. It's the only rag doll."

"All right," Miss Lavender agreed. She smiled at Florabelle over the top of her gold-rimmed glasses as Miss Plum placed the doll on top of the bookcase.

But Florabelle was not very much comforted by Miss Lavender's smile. She watched unhappily from the bookcase while the rest of the dolls were wrapped.

On Christmas morning the dolls would be unwrapped again by laughing little girls who would hug and kiss them and take them into soft, pillowy beds to sleep tight in their arms. But how could it be a merry Christmas for her? Florabelle had been looking forward to it so much, and now she was only a leftover, an extra. Her glass eyes stared at the fire sadly and the clock on the mantel hurried along— *ticktock, ticktock, ticktock...*

The Girl Who Could Talk to Dolls

"What are they doing?" asked the doll with her face to the wall. "I can't see a thing."

"Wrapping the dolls," Florabelle said.

"I wish I could see. You can't imagine how much I miss with my head on wrong. My name is Lily—what's yours?"

"Florabelle."

"That's very nice," said Lily.

For a while the two sat in silence. Florabelle watched Miss Lavender and Miss Plum finish wrapping the dolls. Then the dolls were put back into the brown cardboard box, and the women pushed it across the floor and hid it in the closet. On Christmas Eve, when all the little girls were sleeping, Miss Lavender and Miss Plum would take out the dolls and put them under the Christmas tree.

"There, that's done," Miss Plum said. She took a list out of her pocket and checked off *wrap dolls* with a sharp black pencil.

Then Miss Plum went off to see about some of the other "things to do" that she had written down on her list. Miss Lavender sat down at the table and began to sew angel wings on one of the costumes she picked up from the sofa. The room was very still.

"Now what are they doing?" Lily asked.

"They've finished wrapping the dolls and put them away in the closet," Florabelle said.

"Aren't they going to wrap us?" Lily asked. Her voice was full of longing to be wrapped in Christmas paper and given to some little girl on Christmas morning. "Aren't they going to fix me and wrap me up too?"

"I guess not right now," Florabelle

answered. "We're extra."

"Well, this is just awful," Lily muttered to herself, staring at the yellow flowers twining in the green wallpaper above the bookcase. "This is just awful! What's that? Now what's happening?"

"Some little girls are coming in," Florabelle said.

There had been a knock on the parlor door, and Miss Lavender had called, "Come in." She looked up over her glasses as the door opened.

Five little girls wearing dark blue dresses with white collars, long black stockings, and black shoes with buckles at the sides—all exactly alike—came into the room.

Miss Lavender stood up. "I've been expecting you," she said to the girls. She took them one by one by the shoulder and lined them up in a row in front of the fireplace. "Now, who's missing?" she asked.

"The Angel of Light. The Angel of Love. The Angel of Hope. The Angel of Joy. The Angel of Peace on Earth—ah, now where is the Angel of Glory?"

Just as she spoke, a sixth little girl appeared in the parlor doorway. Her blue dress and white collar were just like the other little girls', and her black stockings and black shoes with buckles at the sides were just the same. But somehow she did not look quite as neat. Her long stockings had wrinkled around her ankles, and her long, straight brown hair fell forward into her eyes.

"Oh, there she is," Miss Lavender said.

"Well, Tatty—come along, dear." She began to hand out angel costumes to the little girls. "Here you are, Mary, and here you are, Emmy—and Cissie—and here's yours, Elizabeth—and this one is Little Ann's—"

One by one the Angels of Light, Love, Hope, Joy, and Peace on Earth took the soft, white angel dresses and pairs of stiff, white net wings. Then Miss Lavender said, "Now take these to the playroom—that will be our dressing room on the night of the program."

"Yes, Miss Lavender." "Yes, ma'am." And the five girls scampered off. Little Ann, the

Angel of Peace on Earth, went last, trailing her long dress along on the floor.

Only Tatty remained. Miss Lavender pulled up Tatty's stockings with a good yank at both knees and smoothed the hair back from Tatty's forehead. Florabelle, the rag doll, watched in surprise as two large brown eyes appeared from under the hair—two eyes staring straight at her.

"Ohhh, Miss Lavender, look at the dolls," Tatty said.

Miss Lavender looked flustered. She and Miss Plum had not meant to leave even these extra dolls where the girls might see them. Miss Lavender pretended to be very busy with the wings on Tatty's costume. "These wings are not very even, I'm afraid," she mumbled to herself.

"Are they your dolls?" Tatty asked.

"Dolls?—dolls?—I don't see any dolls," Miss Lavender muttered. She turned Tatty around and held the costume up to her back to check the wings.

When she let go, Tatty turned around again.

"The dolls on the bookcase," Tatty said. She ran across the room and stretched up as far as she could reach. The top of the bookcase was very high, but Tatty did get hold of one of Florabelle's shoeless feet and pulled her down by one leg.

"Woops!" Florabelle said.

"Woops!" Tatty echoed.

"Um—now—now—" Miss Lavender came over to the bookcase. "These are just some old dolls that need mending and fixing up. They aren't ready to play with yet. See, this one needs shoes. And that other one needs some hair."

"And her head's on backward," Tatty said.

"Yes, her head's on backward," Miss Lavender said. She tried to distract Tatty by holding up the angel costume again.

"When they're fixed up, whose dolls will they be?" Tatty wanted to know.

"Well, I don't know…" Miss Lavender said.

"Oh, Miss Lavender—could they be mine?" Tatty begged. Her hair had begun to fall back across her forehead, and from under the fringe of straggling ends, she stared up at Miss Lavender with such longing expression that Miss Lavender could not think of what to say.

"Well—ahem—" Miss Lavender cleared her throat to give herself time to think. She wished Miss Plum would come in. Miss Plum would know what to do.

"I don't have any dolls," Tatty said. "Oh, couldn't I please have these? I like them so much."

"Oh, now, now." Miss Lavender laughed a little. "Why, how do you know what you'll find on Christmas morning—why, maybe on Christmas morning you will have a doll...." Miss Lavender's voice drifted off. Already she had said too much. But Tatty did not seem to understand.

"Oh, please, Miss Lavender," she begged again.

"Besides," Miss Lavender said, "this one's only a rag doll."

"But I like her," Tatty said. She held

Florabelle tightly and rocked her in her arms. "I like rag dolls *best*. They're so soft to hold."

"I like you too," Florabelle said. She wished she could stay with Tatty forever. What a happy Christmas that would be!

"What's your name?" asked Tatty.

"Florabelle," the rag doll answered, although she did not expect Tatty to hear. Whenever people asked dolls what their names were, it was only to be polite, for they could not hear what the dolls answered.

But Tatty said, "Florabelle? That's pretty."

"My name is Lily," called the other doll from the top of the bookcase.

"Hello, Lily," Tatty said, looking up through her tangled hair at the back of the doll's bald head.

Miss Lavender could only hear what Tatty said. "Now, Tatty," she said, "stop playing; we must get this costume fixed."

Miss Lavender took Florabelle and put her back on the bookcase beside Lily. "Come over by the sofa now, Tatty, and let me see if we can get the wings on your costume right."

Tatty went back to the sofa by the fireplace. But while Miss Lavender held the costume and pinned the wings here and there, she kept looking over at Florabelle and Lily. When the wings were straight, Miss Lavender sewed them onto the costume with strong white thread. At last, she said the wings were finished and Tatty could go.

Florabelle cried, "Oh, don't go — don't go." Tatty stopped in the doorway, holding her costume under her arm, and said, "I'll come back and see you again soon."

Then she was gone, and the parlor door closed behind her.

"What's happening now?" Lily cried. "Has she gone?"

"Yes," Florabelle said, "she's gone."

"Do you think she *will* come back to see us?"

"Oh, I hope so," Florabelle said.

The door opened again, but it was only Miss Plum. Behind her came two girls carrying a box of Christmas-tree lights. Florabelle watched as they began to decorate the tree. The girls wore dark blue dresses with white collars and black shoes and stockings like the little girls who had carried off the angel costumes, but these girls were older and taller —tall enough to reach even the top branches of the Christmas tree.

While the girls were working, Miss Lavender drew Miss Plum aside.

"Tatty wanted those dolls over there. We forgot to put them out of sight. I almost told her she would have her own doll if she could be patient enough to wait until Christmas."

"But what will we do with these two?" Miss Plum wondered.

Then through the window Miss Plum saw a car stopping in front of The Good Day Home. "We'll have to think about the dolls later. Mr. Not So Much is here."

And with that, Miss Lavender clasped her hands together, looking very unhappy and flustered. She followed Miss Plum down the hall to the front door, where a loud knocking could already be heard.

Mr. Not So Much

Florabelle and Lily could hear the sound of the front door opening and voices in the hall and then footsteps coming back along the hall toward the parlor.

"What's happening? What's happening?" Lily asked.

Miss Lavender and Miss Plum appeared in the parlor again, followed by a tall thin man with a long thin face and a long thin nose. He carried his hat in his hand.

"A gentleman has come to visit, I guess," Florabelle said to Lily.

"What does he look like?" Lily wanted to know.

The man had taken off his coat, and Miss Lavender was busy brushing snowflakes off the collar. Miss Plum sat down on the sofa by the fire, and the man took a seat across from her, moving stiffly, as though he thought his legs would break if he bent his knees too deeply.

Mr. Not So Much was on the Board of Directors of The Good Day, and he came once a month to check on things for the other directors.

He looked with disapproval at the girls who were hanging strands of silver icicles on the tree. "Not so much," he said, "not so much." Then he said to Miss Plum, "I hope you saved the icicles from last year. Every penny counts, you know. Can't run things on wasteful ways."

"How true," said Miss Plum. Miss Lavender just smiled. The girls began to roll their eyes and make faces when the grown-ups were not looking. One of the girls put a shiny icicle on her nose and blew it away.

"What does he look like?" Lily asked again.

"He looks very stern," Florabelle said. "He's very thin and very stern-looking, and he is dressed all in black."

"Oh," said Lily. "I think I'm afraid of him."

"How can you possibly be afraid of him when you haven't seen him?" Florabelle wanted to know.

"His voice sounds so cross and mean," Lily said. She lowered her own voice to a whisper, though of course there was no need, since none of the people in the room could hear dolls talk.

"A penny saved, ladies, is a penny earned," the visitor went on. He looked very grave. Then he said, "Too much wood on that fire, ladies. You must understand that we cannot have these spend-thrift ways. Not so much wood, not so much wood."

Miss Lavender and Miss Plum looked toward their little fire — Miss Lavender had just now been thinking that it needed another log. The women had forgotten that Mr. Not So Much was coming today, or they would not have lit the fire at all.

Before Mr. Not So Much could find anything else to complain about, the door opened and one of the girls came in with a tray of tea things that Cook had just prepared.

"These muffins the girls themselves made only this morning," Miss Lavender told Mr. Not So Much proudly. She poured a cup of tea for him and waited to hear what he thought of the muffins.

"Too many raisins," he said. "Can't have that, you know." The girl who had brought in the tray turned pale as Mr. Not So Much looked at her and repeated, "Can't have that, you know. Can't have these wasteful ways. Something will have to be done." Then to Miss Lavender and Miss Plum he said, "A penny saved, ladies, is a penny earned."

"Yes — yes." Miss Plum motioned to the girl to go away *please,* and the girl hurried out of the parlor. She nearly bumped into Tatty and Little Ann, who were coming in to show Miss Lavender and Miss Plum how nice they looked in their costumes. They came running

in, holding up the fronts of their angel skirts so they would not trip. Beneath the gauzy white skirts their black stockings and sturdy black shoes stuck out.

"Now what is this?" Mr. Not So Much rose in his chair as he spoke.

"What is it, what is it?" Lily asked Florabelle. Both dolls heard Miss Plum's answer.

"Why, this is Little Ann," she said, as calmly as she could, "and this is Tatty. Run along now, children." She was wishing Tatty and Little Ann would run along before Mr. Not So Much noticed their costumes—but, of course, he had noticed those the first thing. The costumes were the first thing anyone would notice, for they covered Tatty and Little Ann from head to foot, and behind each girl flapped two large net wings.

"But what *is* this?" Mr. Not So Much repeated. He set down his cup of tea and the muffin with too many raisins. The girls trimming the Christmas tree began to giggle behind their hands.

"Why—these are costumes for our Christmas Eve program," Miss Plum explained. She tried to sound very unconcerned.

"All the girls in the program have one," Tatty said timidly. Miss Lavender and Miss Plum closed their eyes. There was no use worrying now; the worst was out.

"So all the girls in the program have a costume, do they?" Mr. Not So Much said. He stood up, pulled down his vest, clasped his hands behind his back, and began to pace the floor.

"Oh, I *am* afraid of him, I *am*," Lily whispered to Florabelle—and this time Florabelle was not so sure she wasn't afraid too.

"It obviously does no good to talk to you of saving and economizing, ladies. Each time I come," said Mr. Not So Much, "I find fresh evidence of squandering and overspending. Fires burning, lamps lighted in every room, enough ornaments to trim a dozen trees, muffins so full of raisins there's hardly any muffin. Now each girl has a costume, a *cos*—tume." He drew the word out until even the doll Lily, who could not see him, shuddered just to hear. Tatty and Little Ann stared up at Mr. Not So Much, wide-eyed with fright.

"And I suppose," continued the director, looking around for one more fact to prove his case, "I suppose the closet is full to the ceiling with Christmas toys!" With that he swung around and pulled open the closet door.

Little Ann and Tatty in their angel costumes and the girls trimming the tree craned their necks to look into the closet. There was nothing unusual to see — just some umbrellas, Miss Lavender's violin case, and a big brown cardboard box.

"Well, anyway" — Mr. Not So Much closed the closet door — "you know what I mean." The children looked very disappointed that he had not been right.

Miss Lavender and Miss Plum glanced at each other with relief. The director had not asked what was in the box. That would have spoiled everything.

At last Miss Plum said, as politely as she could, "Sir, there are many ways that we do economize. All the girls clean their own rooms; think of the savings there. And some of the girls help with the washing and ironing, and the younger ones help set the table and wipe the dishes."

Mr. Not So Much waved his hand and shook his head.

"There must be some changes, must be some changes," he declared.

But Miss Plum went on. "And Cook is very careful when she does the marketing. Every penny spent on food is repaid by full value, I assure you. And I myself am teaching the girls how to play the piano. Think of the savings there."

"Having a piano at all is pure extravagance," Mr. Not So Much said. He rapped the instrument sharply with his bony knuckles, which set the metronome off—*click click click click click*...

"Stop that thing!" Mr. Not So Much exclaimed. Miss Lavender bustled over, her skirt flouncing around her plump legs, her white curls bouncing. She clapped her hand over the ticking metronome. Tatty drew back fearfully, and Little Ann hid behind Tatty.

"And we are very careful with our wood," Miss Plum went on, though she had turned pale when Mr. Not So Much hit the piano. The piano was her pride and joy. How could they have music for all their nice programs if she could not play the piano while Miss Lavender played the violin? Miss Plum wanted to get the director's mind off the piano as quickly as possible, and the fire was the first thing she thought of.

"We have a fire this afternoon because it is so close to Christmas," she said. "It just seemed the right thing to do."

"Ah—I suppose you will be running off to the shops one of these days to buy yourself a diamond ring—*and* one for every girl because it seems the right thing to do."

At last Miss Plum could think of nothing more to say. Miss Lavender stood rooted by the piano, her hand holding the metronome, her eyes, as round as saucers, fixed upon Mr. Not So Much.

"Ah!" He flung his hands out to show that he

gave up. "It is of no use, ladies." Florabelle thought he was going to say a penny saved was a penny earned, but he said, "Waste not, want not!" Then he put on his hat, picked up his coat, and went out into the hall again.

Miss Plum rose and followed him, and Miss Lavender, still holding the metronome, followed Miss Plum. Trailing after them at a safe distance went Tatty, the Angel of Glory, and Little Ann, the Angel of Peace on Earth.

From the bookcase Florabelle could see Mr. Not So Much pass the window on his way back to his car. The snow was coming down harder now, and he had his head lowered against it, his hand holding on to his hat. The wind whipped his coat out behind him like a great black cape.

"I hope we never meet him again!" said Lily.

A Terrible Thing!

"Well, that's over for another month," Miss Plum said, coming back into the parlor. Miss Lavender came behind her, not fully recovered from the visit.

"Do you think he will make some changes?" Miss Lavender asked. She half-expected the fireplace or the Christmas tree or the piano to suddenly disappear in a puff of smoke.

"He has been saying that for twenty years," Miss Plum reminded Miss Lavender. "And nothing too bad has ever happened."

"Yes, I know," Miss Lavender said.

"Let's not worry about him anymore today," Miss Plum said. "Let's just sit down and finish our tea and eat some muffins. We deserve them after all we've done today."

Miss Plum put two muffins on Miss Lavender's plate and two on her own.

"Very good muffins," said Miss Plum.

"Oh, excellent," said Miss Lavender.

"Let's have another log on the fire," Miss Plum suggested, and Miss Lavender hurried over and put a good extra-big log into the fireplace.

The afternoon had grown quite dark, and flakes of snow were flying against the windowpanes. From somewhere in the rooms above, Florabelle and Lily could hear little girls singing "...*Jingle bells, jingle bells, jingle all the way...Oh, what fun it is to ride...in a one-horse open...sleigh-eigh...*"

"I smell gingerbread baking," Lily said. "At the house where I used to live, the children's mother made gingerbread every Saturday. It smelled so good. She put white icing on, and the children took turns licking the bowl, one each Saturday. I wish I were there now."

Lily's voice faded off, and Florabelle said,

"Don't feel bad, Lily. This seems like a nice place. They will fix your head and get you some hair, and everything will be all right."

"I hope so," the little bald-headed doll answered with a sigh. "I just can't help feeling homesick." Then after a moment she asked, "What was your home like, Florabelle? Before you came here, I mean."

"I never had a home," Florabelle said. "I always lived in a toy store."

"You never had a home?" Lily asked. She was quite surprised.

"No," said Florabelle. "I've always wanted to belong to a little girl, but no one ever bought me. Then one day the toy-store owner took me off the shelf and put me in a drawer behind the counter. He didn't think anyone was ever going to buy me, and his wife said I didn't look very fresh anymore."

"That wasn't a very nice thing to say," Lily interrupted.

"I suppose it was true," Florabelle admitted. "I'd been sitting in that toy store so long, I just didn't look new anymore. I was dusty, and see how my dress has faded."

"I can't see anything but this wallpaper," Lily reminded her. "There are six flowers in each circle, and five leaves on each stem, and eight petals on each flower."

"How did you get to the clock factory?" Lily asked next.

"The toy-store owner donated me, with a big box of other toys, just like those other dolls were donated by children who had new dolls to play with or had grown up and gotten tired of playing with toys."

"That's what happened to me," Lily said. "One day the children's mother said, 'Now let's get together some toys you don't play with much anymore and Daddy will take them to the factory tomorrow.' The children's daddy worked at the clock factory, you see."

"What happened to your hair and your head?" Florabelle asked.

"Well," said Lily, "my hair had been missing for a long time. No one seemed to know where it had gone. It came unglued—wigs sometimes do, you know—and before the children's mother could get around to gluing it back on, it got lost somewhere. Then one day my head began to get loose, and one of the children turned it around backward for fun, and it wouldn't turn back. It's been quite a nuisance —and I don't suppose I look very pretty either, without my hair. It was lovely brown hair, with curls and ribbons."

"It sounds lovely," Florabelle said. "My hair is only yarn."

"Is it?" Lily said. "Well, don't complain. Yarn hair is better than none, I can tell you that. And anything's better than having your head on wrong."

While the dolls were talking, Miss Lavender and Miss Plum finished their tea. Miss Lavender carried away the tray while Miss Plum cleared off the table where they had been wrapping the Christmas dolls and working on the angel costumes. The fire had died out.

The clock on the mantel chimed six o'clock, and Lily said, "Must be suppertime."

"I guess so," Florabelle said. "I can smell

something awfully good cooking somewhere."

Miss Plum gave a last look around the room and caught sight of the two dolls on top of the bookcase. She came over, picked up Lily, and began to examine her head to see if she could twist it around forward again. As she turned the little doll, a trickle of sawdust fell down to the floor. Miss Plum examined Lily more closely and found a place that was coming apart where Lily's smooth pink arm joined her cloth body.

"Hmmm," said Miss Plum, "I hardly think this doll is worth fixing." And to the horror of both dolls, Miss Plum dropped Lily into the wastepaper basket by the table. In she sank among the scraps of wrapping paper and pieces of thread from the sewing basket.

"*Oh—no—wait—wait—*" Lily cried as loudly as she could.

Florabelle cried, "*Oh—oh—don't do that!*"

But of course Miss Plum did not hear the dolls. She looked at the things on the table again and then threw a piece of stationery into the wastebasket. It landed on Lily and covered her like a smooth white blanket.

Lily had fallen on her stomach, so her face was upward. As she stared from the dark sides of the wastepaper basket to the ceiling above, she saw Miss Plum's hand appear again – this time Miss Plum threw in a crumpled-up ball of tissue-paper scraps. It landed right on Lily's face, and now she could see no more. But in a moment she knew that Miss Plum had gone, for she heard a door closing and footsteps fading away along the hall.

Out Into the Night

The next morning Florabelle, the rag doll, saw a beautiful white world through the parlor window. Even the cars creeping slowly along in the street were covered with snow, like frosted cakes, and each branch of each tree was white with snow. *It is like fairyland*, Florabelle thought, *and now the very next day is Christmas*. Although she feared she might not get to be some little girl's Christmas present, Florabelle felt even sorrier for Lily, lying alone in the wastepaper basket.

It was too far from the top of the bookcase to the bottom of the wastepaper basket for the dolls to talk much, but every once in a while Florabelle would shout down, "I'm still here, Lily. Don't worry, everything will be all right."

"*No*—this is the end of me for sure," Lily would call back. Her voice was muffled by the ball of paper lying on her face.

Miss Lavender and Miss Plum came into the parlor in the middle of the morning and brought the girls who had been trimming the tree. Together they all cleaned up the room and set up some folding chairs at one side. They moved the lamps and the big table and chairs away from the windows, so there was a large empty space that would be the stage.

When the parlor was all ready for the Christmas Eve program, everyone went away again. Miss Plum was the last to go. She took out her key and locked the door behind her so that none of the children could get into the parlor and disturb anything before the program.

Slowly the day passed. Steadily the clock on the mantel ticked, steadily it chimed the passing hours. Sorrowfully Florabelle watched the cars and the people going by outside. The people carried Christmas packages and hurried along, smiling and happy. It was the day before Christmas—a wonderful, wonderful day.

But not for Florabelle, or poor Lily in the wastepaper basket.

The afternoon was drawing to a close when Miss Plum came back. Florabelle heard her key at the lock of the parlor door. She came in carrying another brown cardboard carton, which had just come by parcel post for the little girls.

This box was full of smaller boxes, each one stuffed with candy and nuts, and Miss Plum hid them all away in the closet with the big box of Christmas dolls. Then she sat down at the table, took her list out of her pocket, and began to check over the things she had done and the things she had yet to do.

The top of the paper said *trim tree*, and that was checked off. The next thing was *wrap dolls*, and that was checked off. Farther down the list were items such as *oranges and apples for stockings*, and *turkey, stuffing*, and *plum pudding*.

It was a long list, and before Miss Plum got to the end, checking and thinking and making notes to herself in the margin, her head began to nod. At last she leaned back in the chair. Her eyes closed. Her head tipped sideways. The pencil slipped from her fingers, rolled along the floor.

After a while there was a soft knock on the parlor door. When Miss Plum, sound asleep now, did not answer, a face appeared around the door—a tiny face with large dark eyes almost hidden by straggling hair. It was Tatty, hoping to see the dolls. She did not disturb Miss Plum, but tiptoed to the bookcase and reached up for Florabelle.

"I told you I would come back to see you," she said. "Why—where is Lily?"

"Oh, I am so glad you've come," Florabelle cried. "Lily is in the wastepaper basket. She's been thrown away."

"Thrown away?" Tatty said. She held Florabelle closer and tighter, as if she might lose her, too, somehow.

Tatty tiptoed past the table. Miss Plum stirred a little, but went on nodding and dozing. Tatty looked into the wastepaper basket and saw only paper at first. She took the rim of the basket in one hand and shook the basket carefully. The ball of tissue paper rolled away from Lily's face—and she stared up at Tatty from the midst of scraps. Tatty's eyes widened as she stared back down at the doll.

"Oh, dear," Tatty said.

"Can't you help us?" Florabelle pleaded.

Tatty reached into the wastepaper basket and lifted up Lily.

"Poor Lily," she said, hugging her close. The dolls thought it was wonderful for Tatty to be hugging them so tight and loving them so much. They wished they could stay with her forever.

"I'll take you to a toy store!" Tatty said. "We'll get you all fixed up, Lily. Then no one will want to throw you away."

"What about me?" Florabelle begged. "Don't leave me here, please — they'll throw me away next, I know they will.

"They don't like rag dolls," she said to Tatty. "When they first saw me, they said, 'Ugh, a horrid, old rag doll!' "

"Shame on you, Florabelle," Lily whispered. "They didn't say it like that at all."

But Lily spoke very softly, so that Tatty didn't hear. Then Lily said more loudly to Tatty, "Please don't leave Florabelle. She's my friend."

"Well..." said Tatty slowly, looking back and forth from the dolls to Miss Plum, dozing in the chair by the table. "If they really don't like rag dolls, I guess they won't mind if I take you, will they?"

"They'll be very relieved not to have me sitting around," Florabelle said quickly. She was afraid Miss Plum would wake up at any second and stop Tatty from taking her away.

She wanted to belong to Tatty more than anything else in the world.

"All right," said Tatty, "I'll take you with me, for right now, anyway." She began to tiptoe from the room. Miss Plum moved in her sleep but then sank back again, snoring softly into her collar.

In the hall, Tatty got her coat and scarf and mittens from a long closet lined with little coats and scarves and mittens all exactly alike. Below each coat, on the closet floor, was a pair of boots. Tatty put on everything as quickly as she could, and Florabelle and Lily sat waiting on the floor among the boots, worrying. What if Miss Plum woke up and saw they were gone …or if Miss Lavender or one of the big girls came along…or…

And then somebody did come along— Little Ann, the Angel of Peace on Earth, and Mary, the Angel of Light.

"Tatty! What are you doing?" Mary exclaimed. It was time to wash up for supper, not time to be putting on coats and scarves and mittens and boots.

"I have to go out," Tatty said.

"Aren't you ever coming back?" asked Little Ann. She was the smallest of all the little girls. Someone had found a scrap of Christmas ribbon and tied it around her soft yellow hair, but the bow had slipped down over one ear.

"Of course I'm coming back," Tatty said. "I'm just going out for a minute."

"Did Miss Plum say you could go?" Mary asked.

Of course Miss Plum had not said she could go. Miss Plum was sleeping. No one had said she could go.... "I'll be right back," Tatty said.

"Will you be back in time for supper?" Mary asked. She was eating a cookie and her mouth was covered with crumbs.

"I—I don't know..." Tatty hesitated.

It was nearly suppertime now, and she was very hungry. Seeing Mary eating her cookie made Tatty feel even hungrier.

"Don't miss supper," said Little Ann. "We're having everything good, and cake for dessert."

"The cake has pink frosting—this thick," said Mary. She held up her thumb and first finger quite far apart. "We peeked."

"I'll try to be back in time for supper," Tatty said. She was all ready now, and she picked up the dolls.

"Where did you get the dolls?" Mary asked.

"That one doesn't have any hair," said Little Ann.

"I have to hurry," Tatty said. She started toward the big front door.

"Well, good-bye," said Little Ann.

Mary ate the last of her cookie and brushed crumbs from her mouth. "What about the program?" she asked. "You won't miss the Christmas Eve program, will you, Tatty?"

"No, of course not," said Tatty.

As she went to the door, Little Ann and Mary followed behind her. They called after her to hurry back in time to dress up for the program.

Outside on the stoop everything looked very cold and dark. Dusk had fallen, and the streetlights were going on around Butterfield Square. Snowflakes drifted down against the dolls' faces as they waited for Tatty to decide which way to go.

Tatty went down the steps and out to the street. She stopped by the black iron gate and looked both ways.

At last Florabelle said, "Do you know where there is a toy store, Tatty?"

"No," Tatty admitted, "but we'll find one."

And she set off along the darkening street, into the snow.

The Toy Man

Tatty had not walked far before she came to a street lined with stores. Every window was shining with Christmas lights and sparkling with Christmas decorations. There was a shoe store and a card shop, a grocery store and a bakery, a record shop, a dress shop, a book shop, and a candy shop. The street was crowded with people hurrying to finish their errands and get home. It was Christmas Eve, and everyone wanted to be out of the cold and snow, cozy in their warm houses, enjoying their beautiful Christmas trees or wrapping their Christmas gifts.

"Oh, dear," Tatty said to Florabelle and Lily, "I don't see any toy stores—do you?"

Florabelle and Lily looked out from under Tatty's arm. Snowflakes flew in their faces. They melted on Florabelle's green glass-button eyes, and made everything look wet to her, as if she were looking at the world under water.

At the street corner a lady in a long cape stood ringing a brass bell, and in one store window there was a scene of Christmas carolers dressed in old-fashioned clothes. *"Deck the halls with boughs of holly, fa la la la la la la la la ..."* The song came out through a loudspeaker to the people in front of the store.

It was all very bright and lovely to see. Tatty went along looking at all the shop windows and listening to the bells and the songs. She would have liked to have stopped at every window to look more closely at the pretty things, but she wanted to be back before anyone missed her.

"Let's hurry," someone said, jostling past Tatty on the crowded street. "The stores will all be closing soon."

"Did you hear that?" Florabelle called to Tatty. "The stores will be closing soon!"

"I never thought of that," Tatty said. Her dark eyes clouded. "We must find a toy store before it closes."

"There's one!" Lily cried out. "See the dolls and trains in the window!"

At last, there before them was a toy store. But as Tatty ran toward it, a man came to the door and pulled down a shade. A sign read CLOSED in very big letters.

Tatty knocked at the door as loudly as she could, and the shade came up a few inches. The man peeked out at her. Tatty and the dolls heard him clicking back the lock on the door, and a moment later the door opened.

"Why, what's this?" the man asked, for right away he noticed Lily's pink, bald head and he knew that something was wrong. He held the door open, and Tatty stepped in.

"What can I do for you, young lady?" the shopkeeper asked, and Tatty told him about Lily being thrown away because she had no hair and her head was on backward.

"And she has a leak in her sawdust," Florabelle added.

"Yes," Tatty told the man, "a leak in her stuffing."

Poor Lily listened silently. She was embarrassed to have so many things wrong with her. And as though to make matters worse, the toy man himself said, "And she doesn't have any shoes, either."

"Can you fix her?" Tatty begged. "She is such a pretty doll, and I know she will be sad to be thrown away. Her name is Lily."

"Lily, eh?" The toy man took the doll in his large hands, very gently and carefully. Then he lifted Tatty up and sat her down on the counter right beside him so she could see what he was going to do. Florabelle snuggled in Tatty's lap.

First the toy man gave a good yank and took Lily's head off completely. Then with a large needle and stiff thread he sewed her head on right side around.

"Oh, this is such a relief," were Lily's first words.

He looked in a drawer behind the counter and found a wig that was the right size for Lily. It was a wig of black curls, tied at each side with tiny, blue silk ribbons.

"It's even more beautiful than the wig I had before!" Lily exclaimed when she saw it.

The toy man glued the wig firmly in place, took his stiff thread again, and sewed up the hole by Lily's arm where the sawdust was spilling out.

"Now I'm as good as new," Lily said when the sewing was finished. "No one would dream of throwing me away again. See how beautiful I am!"

"Don't be so vain," Florabelle scolded. "Besides, you still don't have any shoes."

"That's right," said Tatty to the shopkeeper. She forgot that he himself could not hear Florabelle or Lily.

"What's right?" he asked.

"She still doesn't have any shoes."

"We can fix that," the man said. He went to one of the shelves and took down a box full of cellophane packages of doll shoes.

"Oh," said Tatty, when she saw this, "I'm afraid I don't have any money."

"I never take money on Christmas Eve," the toy man answered with a wink. He opened one of the packages and put a pair of tiny white shoes with white silk laces on Lily's feet.

"Ohhh—this is more than I expected!" Lily exclaimed. She felt that she was even more beautiful than ever now.

Florabelle was glad to see her friend Lily fixed up so nicely, but she felt a little shabby herself, now that Lily was so elegant. Of all the Christmas dolls, she was the only doll left without shoes.

Almost as if the toy man read her thoughts, he lifted Florabelle from Tatty's lap and said, "My goodness, none of your dolls have shoes, do they?"

"They're not exactly *my* dolls," Tatty said, but the man was shuffling through the box of doll shoes. This time he took out a shiny black pair with tiny black bows on the front. He put these on Florabelle's feet, and she thought no rag doll in all the world had ever had such splendid, shiny shoes.

"Now, how's that?" The toy man set the dolls side by side to take a good look at them. They smiled back as hard as they could and wished he could hear how much they thanked him.

"Tell him how happy we are," Lily said to Tatty.

Tatty said to the toy-shop owner, "They are very happy, and they want to thank you for everything."

"Do they, now?" The man lifted Tatty from the counter and set her on the floor. She put on her mittens, and he handed Florabelle and Lily to her. She tucked a doll under each arm and walked with the man to the door.

"Better hurry along home now, little one," the shopkeeper said. He opened the door for Tatty. "It's Christmas Eve, and you want to get home before it gets any later."

"Yes, sir," said Tatty. She started out, then turned back and said, "I have to hurry to get back in time for the program. I am going to be the Angel of Glory."

The man smiled down at her. "I am sure you will make a very good angel."

"I have a white dress to wear," Tatty said. "And white wings on my back."

"Well, good-bye," the shopkeeper said. He stood in the doorway and watched as Tatty walked away. She turned again to wave, and the toy man waved too. "Merry Christmas," he called.

"Merry Christmas," called Tatty and Florabelle and Lily. They all felt very happy.

But after they turned the corner and the toy store was out of sight, they began to wonder which way to go. All the shops looked alike, and all the streets looked the same. Some of the stores were closed now, and there were not so many people out.

It had grown very dark, and it was much colder. Tatty began to shiver. She held the dolls tightly and tried to think which way would be best to go. She had never been out alone at night before.

"Are we lost?" Florabelle asked. Tatty did not answer.

Where Is Tatty?

Meanwhile, back at Number 18 Butterfield Square, it had been discovered that Tatty was missing.

Her absence would have been noticed much sooner, except that everything was in such a bustle and buzz of excitement and preparation. Cook was busiest of all, fixing Christmas Eve supper. She thought Christmas was the most wonderful time of the year, and she had put a sprig of holly on her apron front. From time to time she looked up from cooking to admire herself in a shiny pot that hung over the stove.

Just before it was time to eat, Cook put a red- and white-striped candy cane in front of every plate at the table — Tatty's too.

In came the little girls with their blue dresses and white collars, black shoes and black stockings. They did not come in very quietly, because it was hard to be quiet when they were so excited about Christmas. They could smell such wonderful smells coming from the kitchen, and Mary had told everyone about the cake with thick icing.

Miss Plum was still attending to some last-minute details in the parlor, but Miss Lavender came in and took her place at the end of the table. Her white curls were freshly combed, and she had even used a little rouge (which she saved for special occasions).

The girls sat down, poking each other and eyeing the candy canes in front of the plates. But one chair was empty; one place had no little girl happy to see a candy cane waiting for her.

And so it was discovered that Tatty was missing.

"Now where's Tatty?" Miss Lavender said. She was a little annoyed that now, of all times, someone should be out of place.

All the little girls turned to look at the empty chair.

"She's gone out, Miss Lavender," Mary said. And everyone looked at Mary.

"A long time ago," said Little Ann.

"Oh, wouldn't you know!" said a big girl named Elsie May, who was twelve and could hardly bear the silly things that the little girls did.

Miss Lavender had begun to look somewhat distressed when Mary said that Tatty had gone out, and when Little Ann said "a long time ago," Miss Lavender looked even more distressed. She took off her glasses and waved them in the air.

"A long time ago? Where did she go?"

But Mary and Little Ann did not know.

"Oh!" Miss Lavender put on her glasses and looked all around the table to be sure that Tatty was not there somewhere after all.

"She just went out by herself," Mary said, shrugging her shoulders and staring at Miss Lavender with her round blue eyes.

Miss Lavender gazed at Mary as though she

could not believe such a dreadful thing.

"She went out *alone*?" Miss Lavender asked. "She went out *alone*—in the *snow*? In this *dark*? Oh, dear—oh, dear—oh, dear."

And she hurried away to tell Miss Plum.

Miss Plum knew exactly what to do, and she went straight to the telephone in the hall. She asked to be connected with the police station. The policeman who answered listened to Miss Plum and then said that he would send someone over at once to find out the details.

When Miss Lavender heard this, she said, "Find out the details? What more details do they need? Our dear little Tatty is out alone on this cold, dark night—oh, our poor dear little Tatty—" And Miss Lavender took off her glasses and dabbed at her eyes with her handkerchief.

"How could she have gone out without asking?" Miss Plum said with a sigh. "Well, now, Miss Lavender, don't worry so. The policeman will be here soon. He will take care of everything. Maybe someone will be able to think of where she might have gone."

In the meantime, the little girls were told to finish up their nice supper and get ready for the program. It seemed best to try to keep everything as nearly normal as possible. Miss Lavender and Miss Plum tried to think of where Tatty could have gone, so they could help the officer when he came.

In the parlor the Christmas-tree lights were turned on, and a fire burned merrily in the fireplace. Soon the audience for the Christmas Eve program began coming in.

There were all the girls who were not in the program.

There were the handyman and his wife.

There was Cook, the holly sprig in her hair now, with her granddaughter, who always came to see the Christmas Eve programs.

There was also a nice old couple who lived across the square and often came to visit, bringing homemade jelly and cookies for the little girls.

The scenery was in place. Large silver cardboard stars hung from the curtains at the sides of the windows, and there was a large cardboard box painted gray and black to look like a great rock. One of the girls was dressed like a shepherd boy, and she was going to sit on the rock. Two other girls were dressed like sheep.

The story of the shepherds abiding in the fields was the first part of the program. Then came the angels, and the last part was the singing of Christmas carols. Miss Plum was going to play the piano, and Miss Lavender was going to play the violin.

Miss Lavender and Miss Plum stood in the parlor doorway. The sight of all the lovely things, the fire burning and the glittering Christmas tree, the silver stars hanging on the curtains, only made Miss Lavender feel worse to think of Tatty out in the cold, snowy night. Beyond the parlor windows, flakes of snow whirled through the glow of the streetlights.

"It's snowing harder than ever," Miss Lavender whispered to Miss Plum. "Harder than ever...oh, our poor little Tatty...."

Lost

Tatty had to admit they were lost. She held Florabelle and Lily tightly and tried not to cry. She wondered if Miss Plum and Miss Lavender had noticed yet that she was gone. She wished they would notice, and come and look for her. But how could they find her? She had wandered a long way from the stores, and no street seemed to be the one that led to Butterfield Square.

Cats went by silently in the snowy streets, and in the windows of houses Tatty could see the bright lights of Christmas trees. Chimes sounded off in the distance somewhere, echoing in the stillness.

"It must be very late," Florabelle said. Snowflakes had melted on her green glass-button eyes again, and her dress and yarn hair were damp with snow.

Lily was smaller and better protected under Tatty's arm, but even so her new black wig was dotted with snowflakes. "Oh, Tatty," Lily said, "I wonder if you've missed your supper."

"I guess I have," Tatty answered. She was very tired and hungry, and she wished she was back where she belonged having a warm supper and getting ready to be the Angel of Glory. She remembered how good Mary's cookie had looked as she stood eating it in the hallway. Little Ann had said they were going to have "everything good, and cake for dessert." "With icing this thick," Mary had said. Tatty felt so hungry she thought she could hardly stand it. It seemed as if she had been walking forever.

At last Tatty and the dolls came to a low stone wall, and beyond they could see a church, its steeple outlined against the dark sky. Lights shone out through the colored glass windows and made beautiful colored pictures on the snow-covered lawn. The chimes they had heard before were coming from this church. Tatty stood for a moment looking across the snow at the tall spire reaching up into the night.

"I'll bet you've even missed the program by now," Lily said sadly.

"I suppose I have," Tatty answered. She was tired and cold and hungry, and she had wanted so much to be the Angel of Glory. It was Christmas Eve and she was lost—who knew how far away she was from Miss Lavender and Miss Plum and all her friends?

People were coming along the street and going into the church for the service. Florabelle said, "Maybe we could ask someone the way to Butterfield Square."

But people were hurrying by, and no one seemed to notice Tatty and the dolls.

"Well, let's just stay here a few minutes anyway and listen to the chimes," Florabelle said. She thought Tatty must be tired from walking so long. It was very beautiful near the church, and it did not seem so lonely there. The snow had finally stopped falling too.

So they remained staring up at the church, listening to the chimes ring out into the night. And as they stood there, a man came walking along and stopped beside them. He, too, was just looking at the church, not going inside to the service.

"Look, Tatty," Florabelle cried. "It's Mr. Not So Much!"

"Is that really him?" whispered Lily. She had been facing the wallpaper when Mr. Not So Much had visited The Good Day. Now that she saw what he looked like, she was more afraid of him than before. Lily thought he looked as mean as he sounded. "Maybe he won't see us," she whispered. "Can't you find somewhere to hide, Tatty?"

But it seemed to Florabelle that Mr. Not So Much was better than nothing, and she said, "Couldn't we just ask him the way back? He must know."

Tatty looked up at the frightening figure beside her, but before she could gather her courage to speak, he turned and walked away.

"Follow him," Florabelle urged.

"Oh, no," begged Lily. "Let's hide, let's hide!"

"Go on, Tatty," Florabelle urged again, "Follow him — hurry — or we'll lose him."

Already Mr. Not So Much was disappearing into the darkness.

"Please, Sir!"

Tatty started running after the tall thin man, but his legs were so much longer than hers and he was walking so rapidly that she could not catch up with him. She ran, stumbling through the snow and bumping into people coming along the street to church.

At last she came up behind him. He had stopped at a corner to wait for the traffic light to change.

"Please, sir," began Tatty in a very tiny, timid voice.

"Go on with you." Mr. Not So Much did not even look at her but waved her off with his hand. Tatty trailed behind him across the street, splashing in the slushy snow. When they were on the other side she tried again, calling as loudly as she could:

"Please, sir!"

Mr. Not So Much turned and glared down. "Well, what is it, what is it?"

"Please, sir," Tatty began again, "I'm from The Good Day Home, sir."

Mr. Not So Much bent down to look at her more closely.

"The Good Day?" he asked. He could see that she was a little girl like the ones at the home, but he had never taken the time to notice what they looked like.

"Yes, sir," Tatty replied. Her nose was beginning to run, and she sniffed and shivered with cold.

"In that case what are you doing *here*?" he demanded.

"I've been out—and now I'm lost," Tatty stammered.

"Did the ladies let you go out *alone*?" he asked.

"Not exactly," Tatty said. "I had something to do, sort of like a surprise..." Her voice trembled and her last words were drowned out by the loud tooting of a bus crossing the intersection.

A car honked back at the bus, and Mr. Not So Much said, "Bah! We can't talk here in the middle of all this noise. Come, follow me."

And he strode off again, muttering to himself about this inconvenient turn of events. Tatty staggered along behind as well as she could, slipping on the snowy sidewalk, trying to keep up.

"Keep going, Tatty," Florabelle said. "Everything will be all right now."

Tatty was out of breath and could not answer. She was sure that she had lost Mr. Not So Much among the people. Then she saw him in front of her again.

Hurrying to catch up once more, she saw that he had stopped and was waiting for her. He reached out and took Tatty's hand. She

held both dolls in the other arm, and now it was much easier to keep up, with Mr. Not So Much holding her securely by the hand. But she still had to run along.

Mr. Not So Much looked down every so often, and Tatty looked up, trying not to be so frightened of him.

Then Mr. Not So Much did another un-expected thing. He stopped again and lifted Tatty up into his arms, dolls and all, and walked along carrying her.

"Oh, oh, oh, oh," gasped Lily, who found her face pressed tight against Mr. Not So Much's shoulder. She thought she would never be the same again.

Whose Dolls Are We Now?

Tatty and Mr. Not So Much, Florabelle and Lily, arrived at the door of The Good Day while Miss Plum was in the parlor explaining the details of Tatty's disappearance to the policeman. Miss Lavender was standing beside her, listening anxiously.

"She is seven years old," Miss Plum was saying, "and she is wearing a blue dress and a dark blue coat."

The children had given up waiting for the program to start. They were clustered around the piano, and Elsie May picked out "Jingle Bells" with one finger to show the other girls how clever she was.

Miss Plum was interrupted by a knock at the door. She excused herself to the policeman and stepped over to the front door. When she opened it and saw that it was Tatty home safe and sound, she took her into her arms at once and called, "Miss Lavender! Miss Lavender! Tatty's here."

Miss Lavender came flying out of the parlor. All the girls came clattering along, except one small girl who had been waiting for her chance to have a turn at the piano; she stayed behind to see if she could play "Jingle Bells."

After a great many exclamations and explanations, and then more explanations and exclamations, Miss Plum remembered the policeman. He had stepped aside to get out of the way of all the commotion and was holding his hat in his hand.

"Oh," Miss Plum said. "We won't be needing you after all!"

Miss Plum and Miss Lavender tried to thank

Mr. Not So Much, but he only brushed them aside and said, "Not so much chatter. Not so much foolishness." Then he went into the parlor and found the little girl who had stayed behind to play "Jingle Bells." He frowned at her from his great height and said, "Not so much noise, please."

At last everyone went back to getting ready for the program. Tatty was rushed into the kitchen to have a very fast supper and then rushed into her bedroom to put on her angel costume.

Miss Lavender put Florabelle and Lily on top of the piano, and there the dolls had a good view of the program. They thought they had never had such an exciting time in all their lives, and they took turns admiring each other's new shoes and remarking how things had worked out so nicely.

"I was never really worried a bit," Florabelle said. "I *knew* everything would be all right."

"I was never worried either," Lily said, "Except…"she paused. "Except, whose dolls are we now?"

Before Florabelle could think of an answer, Miss Plum clapped her hands for attention. It was time for the program to begin.

When it was their turn, the six little girls who were angels came in from the hall where they had been waiting and peeking through the parlor door. They took their places by the curtains decorated with silver cardboard stars.

Tatty was at the very end of the line. How happy she looked now; no tears or sniffly nose or pinched cold fingers and frozen cheeks. Her hair was combed and held back by the white ribbon. Her long angel dress covered everything but the very tips of her small black shoes. To Florabelle and Lily she looked like the most beautiful little girl in the world.

Miss Plum began to play "Silent Night" very softly on the piano.

"I am the Angel of Light," Mary said, "Heaven and Earth are full of my radiance."

One by one the little girls said their lines:

"I am the Angel of Love, bringing to everyone my gifts of Hope, Joy, and Peace on Earth."

"I am the Angel of Hope. You may find me wherever you hear voices singing the carols of Christmas."

"I am the Angel of Joy. You may see me upon each face touched with the wonder of Christmas."

"I am the Angel of Peace on Earth," said Little Ann. "I live in the hearts of all good people, and wherever a heart receives me, there is Christmas."

Then it was Tatty's turn.

"I am the Angel of Glory," said Tatty, "filling all the Earth with singing and rejoicing and praise to God on Christmas and forever."

Miss Lavender dabbed at her eyes with a handkerchief, and Miss Plum sat up a little straighter at the piano as she, too, blinked a tear back. Mr. Not So Much, who had decided to stay for the program, as long as he was there, took out his handkerchief and blew his nose.

Merry Christmas

Later that night, when the guests had gone home and all the little girls had gone to bed, Miss Plum and Miss Lavender got out the presents that were hidden in the closet. They put the presents into the twenty-eight stockings hung around the parlor. A full row of stockings was hung by the fireplace. The rest were hung on doorknobs and chair backs.

Into each stocking went an orange and an apple and a little box of candy and nuts. Then in went a new box of crayons and a coloring book all rolled up like a tube so it would fit into the stocking. Then into some stockings went whistles, and into some stockings rubber balls, and into some stockings toy pipes for blowing bubbles.

The clock on the mantel ticked on and on and on. Outside, the streets and yards of Butterfield Square lay soft and white and gleaming. Even the wind had sighed itself away to nothing.

The fire in the parlor burned lower and lower, and at last Miss Plum and Miss Lavender had filled every stocking. Then they went to the closet one more time and dragged out the big cardboard box of Christmas dolls.

"What will we do with *these* dolls?" Miss Plum said. She took Florabelle and Lily down from the piano and held them out at arm's length.

"Please give us to Tatty! Please give us to Tatty!" the dolls called. But of course Miss Lavender and Miss Plum could not hear them.

After a minute Miss Lavender said, "Tatty

liked them so much. But I suppose it wouldn't be fair to give Tatty two extra dolls, would it?"

"No, I suppose not," Miss Plum said.

"But we could give her the rag doll for her Christmas doll," Miss Lavender said, "instead of one of those others. Tatty seemed to like it so much."

"And this other little doll would have been thrown away if Tatty hadn't fixed her up," Miss Plum said. "I don't think any of the other girls would mind if we let Tatty keep her too—do you?"

"No, I'm sure the other girls wouldn't mind," Miss Lavender agreed.

She went over to the table and took the wrapping paper from the drawer. Florabelle and Lily were laid together side by side, and rolled up in soft white tissue paper. Then they were wrapped in bright red-and-green Christmas paper and tied with a big piece of ribbon. Miss Lavender and Miss Plum set the package aside in a special place so they would be sure it was given to the right girl.

"Now we have an extra Christmas doll," Miss Lavender reminded Miss Plum. Again the two ladies stopped to think. They looked at all the red-and-green packages lying in the cardboard box, and then Miss Plum snapped her fingers.

"We will give the extra doll to Cook's little granddaughter!"

"What a good idea," said Miss Lavender. "Won't Cook be pleased." She took one of the Christmas dolls and set it beside Cook's Christmas present, which was a box of pincushions and bookmarks and calendars made for Cook by the twenty-eight little girls.

"I'm so glad you thought of that," Miss Lavender said to Miss Plum. Miss Plum always seemed to know just the right thing to do.

Then they took out all the other wrapped Christmas dolls in the cardboard box and set them under the Christmas tree, where the girls would find them Christmas morning.

When Miss Lavender and Miss Plum were finished it was very late. They went up to their beds very tired and very happy. The parlor was dark and silent. And then slowly the sky began to grow light…and lighter…and lighter …until it was Christmas morning, and all the Christmas dolls could hear the excited cries of little girls in the bedrooms above, and the sound of their steps

running
down
the
stairs!

Into the parlor they burst, following Miss Plum and Miss Lavender by just a few seconds. The little girls ran to find their stockings, and then each girl picked a package from under the tree.

"Your package is here on the sofa, Tatty," Miss Lavender whispered, and she led Tatty aside to where Florabelle and Lily lay wrapped and tied with Christmas ribbon.

"My wish has come true!" Tatty exclaimed, as she tore away the paper and saw Florabelle and Lily.

"Our wish has come true too," Lily and Florabelle said. They had so much to say to her—and they had all the time they needed to say it, for now they were going to belong to her, to their dear, dear Tatty.

"Don't eat all your candy before breakfast," Miss Plum reminded the girls. But she was not sure that anyone was listening to her. They were all so busy showing each other their dolls and examining the presents tucked into their Christmas stockings.

Cook came in and opened her package and said she had always wanted some pincushions and bookmarks and calendars. Then Miss Lavender and Miss Plum opened their packages and found that they, too, had their whole next year's supply of pincushions and bookmarks and calendars—and also some nice chocolate fudge that Cook had helped the girls make as an extra surprise.

Later that day, the girls lined up their Christmas dolls along the window seat and went out to play in the snow. The dolls sat and talked among themselves, mostly of how glad they were to be unwrapped at last.

The fire sputtered and a log shifted and sent bright flames shooting up for a moment. From outside could be heard the shouts of the girls playing in the snow.

Florabelle and Lily sat close together on the window seat. They felt very peaceful and happy and drowsy.

"I wonder what will happen to Tatty when she grows up," Lily said.

"She will probably have some little girls of her own someday," Florabelle said. "She will be a beautiful lady with earrings and high heels. She'll probably forget she ever was a little girl who could talk to dolls."

Lily rested her new black curls against the window frame and watched the flickering firelight. "You may be right," she said very softly "You may be right."

The Christmas tree sparkled, and the fire on the hearth burned warm and bright.

It was a lovely, lovely Christmas.